How to Use this Book

Throughout this guide book you will find several "badges" on the listings of stables. These badges help you to find the most suitable riding destination quickly based on your preferences, budget, experience and wish-list.

VERIFIED BADGE

A Verified Badge is only given to stables which the Equestrian Adventuresses Team has personally visited and verified the welfare of the horses with their own eyes.

Travel Badges Key:

Budget Badges:

Tours for $1,000 or Less

Tours between $1,000 - $3,000

Tours between $3,000 - $5,000

Luxury Tours $5,000+

Best Time of the Year to Visit:

All Year

 Nov-Feb

Mar-Oct

June-July

Travel Badges Key: (Continued)

Topography:

Mountains

Forests

Beaches

Jungle

Deserts

Meadows

Historical Sites

Rivers / Lakes

Villages

Riding Experience:

Beginners   Intermediate   Experienced   Non-Riders Welcome

Pace of Riding:

Mostly Walking

Variety

Fast Riding

Time in Saddle Per Day:

 1-3 hours   3-5 hours   5+ hours   variety

Travel Badges Key: (Continued)

Weather:

 Sunshine

 Humid

 Rain

 Snow

 Plan for Anything

Ridng Disciplines:

English   Western   Show Jumping   Endurance

Dressage   Polo   Natural Horsemanship

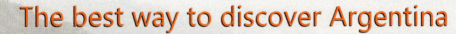

Interested in Traveling the World on Horseback But Don't Know Where to Start?

What You'll Learn:

- How to Speak the Horse Language in ANY country
- How to be more confident on the ground and in the saddle with horses
- How to travel solo confidently
- Strategies to achieve your goals--no matter how big your dreams are
- How to gain your horse's trust and build their confidence
- Mastering your own body language
- What is "Energy" and how does it influence your horse
- How to stay safe while traveling as a solo woman
- How to read situations
- Effective strategies to turn your goals, ideas & dreams into ACTIONABLE PLANS
- And much, much more!

Learn from the comfort of your own home with this simple online video course!

https://linktr.ee/equestrianadventuresses

INTRODUCTION

EQUESTRIAN ADVENTURESSES

Welcome to the Equestrian Adventuresses Travel Guide 2020-2021 Series.

 We have worked hard to dig deep and find the top horse riding destinations around the world for you to book your next horse riding expedition. We update the information in this Travel Guide Series every year so please make sure you have downloaded the most recent edition. You can find out more on our website: www.equestrianadventuresses.com

If you are the owner of a riding stable or holiday destination and are not on this list and would like to be featured in next years catalog please get in touch with us.

If you book a riding holiday or use any of the stables in this directory, please share your feedback, photos and stories with us! You may email us on our website or join our Facebook Group - Equestrian Adventuresses to let other adventuresses know that you enjoyed your experience!

Happy Trails!
Krystal Kelly
Equestrian Adventuresses Founder

Last year's catalog, **Horse Riding in Every Country** was well recieved by our Equestrian Adventuresses Community. Because of the catalog, countless of horse riders around the world have traveled and ridden at some pretty spectacular places such as Dubai, Croatia, Bosnia and Herzegovina and even Rwanda!

The Horse Riding in Every Country Catalog was designed to be like a phone-book. It's a handy resource of endless listings where you'll find over 400+ stables in over 180 different countries. (If a country has horses, we found a place for you!) This ultimate equestrian's "phone book" of stables took our team over 3 months to create. Get your Free Copy at catalog.equestrianadventuresses.com/catalog-freebie

And so at the request of our community we have now decided to release a series of "Travel Guide Books." Because for many beginners and those new to traveling the world on horseback a phonebook list wasn't enough. These Travel Guide series are designed to dive deeper and give more specific information about a variety of countries and unique places to ride horses so that you don't have to feel overwhelmed at researching all 180 countries!

DISCLAIMER

Although we did our best to include relevant horse riding stables for experienced riders, it is simply impossible for us to physically visit each and every stables in the world in order to verify them.

Please use caution when booking any horse riding expedition without doing the proper research and vetting of the people, horse care and accommodations. It is your responsibility to look at their website's thoroughly, check the reviews, and post in our Facebook Group: Equestrian Adventuresses if you are looking to see photos and hear firsthand reviews of the destination you're interested to visit.

Interested in Traveling the World on Horseback But Don't Know if You Are a Confident Enough Rider or Solo Traveler?

Check out the Equestrian Adventuresses Master Class for access to our complete online video course. In this course you will learn how to speak the horse's language in order to travel and ride confiendly with a variety of horses and disciplines around the world. You'll also unlock videos encompassing women's travel safety tools, goal setting tactics and all the skills you need to be a true Equestrian Adventuress!

Find out more at: www.EquestrianAdventuresses.com

Learn from Krystal at:
https://linktr.ee/equestrianadventuresses

Learn from Krystal how to "Speak the Horse Language" no matter what country you travel to with the Equestrian Adventuresses Masterclass!

https://linktr.ee/equestrianadventuresses

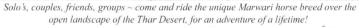

Ride in
Slovenia with
Horses on Breg

www.horsesonbreg.si

The best way to discover Argentina

Ampascachi Horse Riding Holidays
https://ampascachi.com

Table of Contents

New Mexico

The International Balloon Festival, the Spanish and Indian Folk Art markets, the Roswell UFO Festival, the New Mexico State Fair, Rodeos, the Festival of the Cranes... New Mexico has year round festivals and events celebrating the arts, culture and food. In fact, there are so many festivals that it's easy to get overwhelmed at knowing which one's to plan your trip around! Make sure you speak to some locals or do a little research in advanced so you can plan your visit during your "must-see festival" events list. You may even need to plan multiple trips to this beautiful state!

Your horse looks up at the sea of hot air balloons floating above. You are astounded at your horse's calmness as you both watch the serenity of the balloons. The sun is beginning to set and the sky is dancing with an array of colors, adding more to the picture-perfect setting. You take a deep breath as you sink deeper into the saddle. Life simply couldn't get any better than this...

New Mexico is a magical place just calling out to horse riding enthusiasts to explore. New Mexico is known as the land of enchantment and when one gazes at the glowing hues of various earth, pink and reddish tones on the buttes and the mountains covered with pine trees, it is clearly enchanting. The scenery is stunning, the sunsets magical and the western landscapes surreal. Horseback riding trails can take one over the mountains, through rivers, along sandy trails in the White Sands National Monument and through magnificent buttes.

Another very unique aspect of this state is that it has numerous hot air balloon festivals throughout the year to enhance the already magical feel of this grand place. To make it even more enticing one can find food and wine festivals to try the local specialties. Culinary delights, culture and great food can be found in the picturesque towns of Santa Fe and Taos. Albuquerque is the door to this magical kingdom and a great place to start your adventures. You can fly in here and find lodging and good food nearby.

Finally, to really capture the essence of the culture it is a great idea to attend one of the native American events with ancient Indian rituals. Ancient ruins can be seen at Jamez historic site.

Explore Ithe History Museums

Learn about the Native American
Arts and Festivals

Things to Do:

New Mexico also has many outdoor adventures such as hiking, rafting, kayaking, fishing, skiing, biking, camping and of course horse riding!

Some of the things to do include visiting the caves at Carlsbad Caverns, exploring the White Sands National Park and relaxing at one of the many natural Hot Springs. You can also trek the Continental Divide Trail (CDT) or visit the Chaco Culture National Historical Park. One of the most stunning natural beauties is the Kasha-Katuwe Tent Rocks and it's a great place to see the unique cone-shaped rock formations. Whether you want to experience food and wine overlooking stunning views or adventurous nature activities, New Mexico is always there to deliver.

Highlights:

If you want to feel like a cowboy or a cowgirl riding into the old west then this is a unique place to discover. The other big highlight of New Mexico? Chile. That's right, be sure to get used to eating a variety of Chile in an assortment of local cuisines. You'll hear locals asking things like, "Red, Green or Christmas?" This question may confuse a lot of outsiders, but it simply means, "what kind of Chile do you want in your food?" (Christmas means you want both red and green chiles, hence Christmas...)

Highlights: (Continued)

You'll also be in Turquoise heaven and you simply cannot leave without visiting a local artisan market featuring this beautiful stone. Lots of New Mexico's small towns and cities were designed for horse-drawn wagons so it's best to explore the cozy streets, unique architecture, art galleries and colorful murals on foot.

Highlights: (Continued)

Santa Fe is a highlight in of itself. Within the city you can explore Canyon Road, the prime hotspot for art lovers. There are also several museums including the Museum of International Folk Art, the New Mexico Museum of Art or the New Mexico History Museum. Set some time aside for the Santa Fe Farmers Market, go skiing or check out the Cathedral Basilica of St. Francis of Assisi. History buffs or architecture lovers will delight at the breathtaking Roman cathedral. You can also see ancient cave dwellings and other stone structures at the base of the Frijoles Canyon belonging to the ancestors of the Pueblo People.

Where to Ride

Enchantment Equitreks

A unique horseback riding experience in New Mexico. Our diverse culture, stunning landscapes, and exceptional cuisine makes us a once in a lifetime destination.

We offer all inclusive vacation packages, EquiYoga retreats, Balloon Fiesta, Rodeo, Wine Festival specialty rides, and volunteer opportunities. Named a top destination for solo women travelers by Equitrekking.

Visit our website for information on our work with rescue horses.

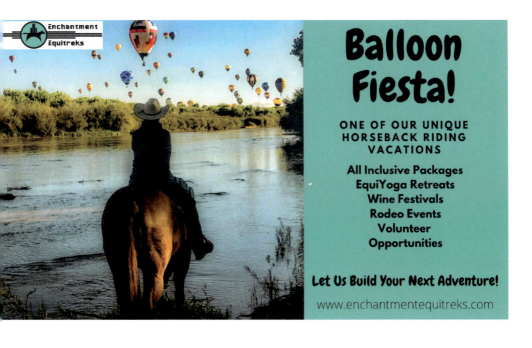

How to Book Your Trip:

Location: New Mexico - United States of
America
www.enchantmentequitreks.com

Enchantment Equitreks:

April - Oct

1-3 hours   3-5 hours   5+ hours   variety

Beginners   Experienced

Intermediate   Non-Riders
                             Welcome

English   Western   Show Jumping   Endurance

Dressage   Polo   Natural
                             Horsemanship

Types of Horses Used:

All of our horses are rescues. Breed varies. No gaited horses.

California

This is a very large State with a variety of terrain options for Equestrian Adventuresses to explore. Most people think of Hollywood, movie stars, beaches and the Golden Gate Bridge in San Francisco. What most do not realize is that there are Coastal mountains with giant Sequoia trees, Calaveras Redwood Tree's and beautiful forest's in two different mountain ranges as well as Dessert sand and beaches.

Pro Tip

San Francisco is one of those cities that a lot of people seem to love. Europeans especially adore the charm and vibe that this city brings. Because of the major International airport, consider flying to California via San Francisio (rather than LA) and spend a couple of days exploring the city.

There are valleys, cliffs along the beach, many lakes, rivers, rolling hills and most importantly for Equestrian Adventuresses, trails to ride horses on. You can find Western riding, English riding, Polo, and Endurance riding.

Now for your other activities in between finding some trails to explore, you have options. Do you want to explore some wineries in Napa, Sonoma, Pismo Beach or Santa Barbara and taste some very delicious wines while strolling along or having a picnic in a beautiful vineyard? Or do you want to watch the sunset on the beach from atop of a horse? Kayaking, paddle boarding on a lake or rafting down a river are also options. How about a hot air balloon ride over the Napa Valley?

Mountains, beaches, desert, cities, forests, National Parks... California has it all...

Having a vehicle is a must if you want to take in all that this State has to offer and do it in California style, which is at a leisurely pace. Did you say you like great food? Well, you have so many options depending on which area you go to. However, you have to have a Carne Asada (steak) taco from a Mexican Food truck, sushi, fresh salads galore, strawberries, cherries and a plethora of other fruits and an In N Out burger and fries.

These are just a few of the things you must experience. Most of all, whether you are just a horse person and don't like people, you must do some people watching. The diversity in parts of California adds to the unique culture that one cannot just explain. You are sure to find some interesting experiences, but remember your travel safety. This is not your small town culture, even in the small towns. What do I mean? You will see.

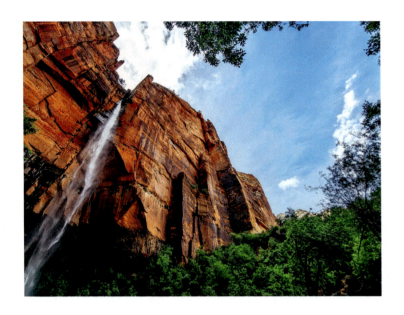

California has nine national parks that include some of America's most incredible landscapes. The Golden State also has 280 state parks if you want a more local feel without the International travelers.

Yosemite National Park

Yosemite has grand granite and alpine scenery, but there can be crowds during holidays. So you can enter through alternative routes. Or you can go to Mount San Jacinto State Park and take in its massive granite peak. There is access to the the summit by riding the Aerial Tramway to Mountain Station, then you can set out on foot. Or you can drive to the village of Idyllwild to explore other park trails, which also includes a section of the 2,650-mile Pacific Crest Trail.

Death Valley and Joshua Tree National Parks

Death Valley and Joshua Tree national parks have amazing landscapes. You can also go to Anza-Borrego Desert State Park, east of San Diego. This park has the largest tract of state-preserved land, Anza-Borrego spans more than 600,000 acres.

Take a hike into Borrego Palm Canyon, which is fed by underground springs. Then walk through a steep-walled canyon at The Slot. At sunset, visit Fonts Point to see the Borrego Badlands for an amazing view of golden hills and sand-colored arroyos.

California

 April - November

Where to Ride

Horse N Around Trail Rides
horsenaroundtrailrides.com

San Diego Horse Trail Riding
sandiegohorsetrailriding.com

Central Coast Trailrides
cctrailrides.com

Crescent Trail Rides
crescenttrailrides.com

Redwood Trails Horse Rides
redwoodhorserides.com

Western Trail Rides
westerntrailrides.org

Western Trails Horseback Riding
ridenorco.com

S&D Horseback Riding
sunshineanddaydream.com

Florida

With millions of acres of public lands, Florida has one of the best trail systems in the United States. From beach rides and day jaunts to deep-forest treks. Perhaps the biggest draw for Equestrian Adventuresses is that you can gallop on the beach, take a swim or paddle board around and then relax under the shade to rest until your ready for a fabulous meal or mixed refreshing drink. Ah, doesn't the warm sand feel good under your toes and the sound of the waves just rest your mind? Yes, you can have it all in Florida if you are wanting a warm place to go with lots of tropical feel, good food, interesting and unique wildlife such as Manatees, exotic birds, dolphins and alligators.

There are the popular tourist places to go if you want to do wild people watching as well. Such as, Disneyworld in Orlando or the beaches and clubs in Miami. The Everglades National Park in Southern Florida is a unique habitat to explore that is best done on a pontoon boat.

Driving out through the Keys is a scenic excursion to get your tropical fix through the multitude of islands and vast ocean views. You can paddle board in Palm Beach to catch a glimpse of a huge Manatee slowly drifting by. On the west side of Florida you can find the beach, waterways and marinas with beautiful yachts such as in Sarasota. There is so much coastline to explore and as you head north you will find southern hospitality in quaint fishing towns.

So much wildlife to see!

Having a vehicle to explore this vast state is a must and gives you the freedom to roam. Just don't forget the sunscreen and check the weather for the best times of the year to explore.

Florida

November - May

Where to Ride

Florida Horseback Trail Rides
floridahorsebacktrailrides.com

Cactus Jack's Trail Rides
floridahorseriding.com

American Horse Trails
americanhorsetrails.us

Myakka River Trail Rides
myakkatrailrides.com

Hidden Palms Ranch Trail Rides
hiddenpalmsranch.com

Orange Blossom Trail Rides
orangeblossomtrailrides.com

Lazy H Ranch
lazyhranch.net

Choyce LLC
choycellc.com

Colorado

Colorado is known worldwide for the great Rocky Mountains that run thru the center of the state. You can snow ski at several famous resorts in Aspen, Vail and Breckenridge. However, the rest of the year these mountains are great for hiking, mountain biking, swimming in numerous lakes and driving up passes for stunning views.

Pro Tip

A wonderful feature to Colorado is that there are natural Mineral Hot Springs in various parts of the State. Some of them are Steamboats Strawberry Park, Glenwood, Pagosa Springs, Dutton Hot Springs and Mt. Princeton.

Horse riding adventurers can find Dude Ranches and various trekking excursions to enjoy the mountains in the Rocky Mountain National Forrest, and sand dunes at the Great Sand Dunes National Park in Southern Colorado. The Continental Divide trail a challenge one of our Equestrian Adventuresses conquered and is just the sort of adventure for some of our more spirited equestrians.

Many Native American Tribes have ceremonies in Colorado and there are many Pow Wow ceremonies that you can attend to see and feel the energy of the cultures. Mesa Verde is the home of the Ancestral Puebloans whom built amazing cliff dwellings in the 12th century that are a must see when in Colorado.

The perfect place for a gallop... Photo Credits: Equestrian Dream Egypt

Get Entranced by the Colors of Nature.

Of the historic sites and activities that are perfect for scenery and getting a feel of the Old West, you can ride a historic train, such as the Durango-Silverton Railroad. Another well known historic place from the Stephen King book, The Shining, is the Stanley Hotel in Estes Park. The town is great to visit and is one of the gateways to the Rocky Mountains.

Before leaving this beautiful area you might want to go to Boulder to get a feel for the hippie vibe there and go to a marijuana dispensary if that is of interest to you.

The Red Rocks Natural Amphitheater is also known worldwide for the great acoustics and setting for attending concerts. You may want to plan your trip to Colorado with a concert of your preference to attend, it is simply fantastic.

One of the top features in the entire state are the numerous breweries and distilleries. Everywhere you go, you are sure to find some unique beverages that offer a variety for every palette. Coloradans are friendly outdoors oriented people that will gladly welcome you.

Colorado

 March - May,
September - October

Where to Ride

A&A Historical Trails Stables
aastables.com

Elk Heart Outfitters Trail Rides
elkheartoutfitters.com

Bear Mountain Stables
bearmtnstables.com

Action Adventures Trail Rides
ride.actionadventures.net

Rusty Spurr Ranch
rustyspurr.com

Bear Creek Stables
bearcreekstablescolorado.com

High Country Trails
highcountry-trails.com

Cowpoke Corner Corral
khorses.com

New York

The Seneca Lake Wine Trail puts you in the midst of cascading waterfalls, breathless lake views and rolling glacier carved hills. Breathe in the fresh air and breathtaking views that make the Finger Lakes National Forest so beautiful. The Finger Lakes Region of west/central New York State has 11 lakes with more than 650 miles of shoreline. This region also has the wine country for those wanting to do some wine tasting and relaxing.

Most Equestrians don't think about the State of New York when they plan to go horse trekking in the United States. However, consider the contrast this state has. New York City with its large supply of culture, food, entertainment and history and then upstate New York, with the Adirondack Mountains, located in eastern upstate New York. These mountains are an all-season, year-round vacation destination with scenic views, skiing, many trails for hiking or riding, lakes and rivers to enjoy many water sports on. Further north is Niagara Falls.

Niagara Falls is a mesmerizing experience in itself. Simply a once in a lifetime experience. Take a boat or helicopter tour to get the full view and then enjoy a gourmet meal at sunset with a view of the falls.

The Catskill Mountains lie in southeastern New York State. The area is known for the Catskill Forest Preserve, with its rich wildlife and hiking trails, and ski resorts including Hunter Mountain and Belleayre Mountain.

Believe it or not there are beaches in New York as well. Coney Island is a popular spot with a carnival, food stalls and playtime on the beach, but you can also find some more relaxed beaches to ride a horse along. New York also offers an enriched experience with ranches, farms, towns, retreats, and a variety of tucked away places with miles of trails to explore. People in this state are fully aware of the need to unplug, regroup, get therapy and relaxation and there are a number of places that provide what you need here.

New York

May - June
September - November

Where to Ride

Cimarron Ranch cimarronranchny.net

Westchester Trail Rides
westchestertrailrides.com

Fox Hill Farms Inc
foxhillfarms.net

Juckas Stables, Inc.
juckasstables.com

Lakewood Stables Ltd
mynyec.com

Nativity Riding Academy
nativity-riding-academy.com

Babylon Riding Center, Inc.
babylonridingcenterny.com

Kensington Stables
kensingtonstables.com

Wyoming

People visit Wyoming from all over the world to visit the famous Yellowstone National Park and Grand Teton National Park. Along with these massive parks there are vast forests to explore. Equestrian Adventuresses are in their element in this state. Because there is so much space it is important to have a vehicle to explore and get to the various destinations.

The amazing natural world of Wyoming cannot be captured in pictures the way it feels to be outside in the breeze, smelling the trees and gazing at the massive rocks and peaks.

Viewing while riding a horse is always the most amazing way and why as Equestrians we can get a more personal view than the thousands of tourists stuck on the roads. This is where we play the best!

Riders have the option of going to working, traditional or dude ranches for various types of riding and experiences. You can experience the cowboy way of life on a Trail Ride, at a Guest Ranch or on a Pack Trip. If you want to learn how cowboys do roping, team penning or you want to help on a cattle drive, Wyoming is where you can do it. There are thousands of miles to explore and you can even play polo!

Outdoor activities are the primary focus in Wyoming and it offers numerous other activities to enjoy before or after an equestrian adventure. Some of the activities are: Camping, stargazing, All Terrain Vehicle and off roading, fishing, float trips and rafting, golf, Hot Springs, mountain biking, rock climbing, wildlife viewing and ziplining.

Knowing how great it is to soak in Hot Springs after a riding adventure, here is a list of places to go:

Hot Springs State Park in Thermopolis, Star Plunge, Hellie's TePee Pools, Saratoga Hot Springs Resort, Saratoga Hobo hot pools and Boiling River Hot Springs.

Relaxing afterwards can also be done at some of the Breweries, Distilleries and a Meadery.

When you do plan to visit this state, give yourself at least two weeks to take it in and truly feel the energy of the grand nature you will encounter.

Wyoming

 June - August

Where to Ride

Willow Creek Horseback Rides
fishjacksonwyo.com

CODY YELLOWSTONE
codyyellowstone.org

Wyoming Summer Pack Trips
wyomingsummerpacktrips.com

Swift Creek Outfitters -
Teton Horseback Adventures
horsebackadv.com

Yellowstone Wilderness Outfitters
yellowstone.ws

Rockin' M Horseback Rides
rockinmhorsebackrides.com

Lazy L&B Ranch
lazylb.com

Canyon Horse Corral
yellowstonenationalparklodges.com

Oregon

Made up of seven diverse regions, Oregon has the ocean, mountains, valleys, high desert, cities, small towns, and almost everything in between.

First there is the wild blue Pacific Ocean with vast beaches in towns like Florence and Seaside, interspersed with cliffs, rock crags and coastal mountains in the middle of the coast in Waldport and Newport. Then, the Columbia River Gorge splits Oregon from Washington with a spectacular river that one can Jet boat or take a small cruise on. On the southern coast there are sand dunes, along the mid coast and in the east there are mountains, rivers and beautiful valleys. In the east is the Mighty Mt. Hood with snow skiing, hiking and many outdoor sports.

Near Portland you can go wine tasting in the Willamette Valley and taste Pinot Noir that is earthy, find a luscious fruit forward red wine or find a tasty and refreshing white wine. The wine region is vast with lots of varietals. For those that love beer and Ales there are also many micro- breweries where you can taste flights of one of a kind brews.

Multnomah Falls along the Columbia River are a breathtaking site where you can feel the mist from the falls while on one of the many trails to explore. Crater Lake is another vast natural area with views galore.

Popular spots for horseback riding and treks are along the coast where you can ride through the coastal mountains and onto a vast open beach. There are many places to ride along the coast. In the mountains you can find some treks through the higher elevations with views of Mt. Hood.

Spring in Oregon, is when dozens of bird species and thousands of gray whales make their spring migration. This is a great time to visit when you get to see these spectacular animals. You can see them from the coast or take a boat on a whale watching tour. Fall is generally the mildest in terms of weather on the coast, so if that is your destination and you don't want the bloom of spring you will find this is the time to go.

Any time of year is great to see the grand Elk wandering through Valleys between the mountains. You will want to check the routes of where these majestic animals graze.

Wherever you roam in Oregon you will find a relaxing and mystical zone awaits you.

Oregon

 June - August

 Mild Temperatures in Summer

Where to Ride

Central Oregon Trail Rides
centraloregontrailrides.com

Smith Rock Trail Rides
smithrocktrailrides.com

Oregon Beach Rides
oregonbeachrides.com

Double Mountain Horse Ranch
ridinginhoodriver.com

Perrydale Trails
perrydaletrails.com

Juniper Trails Horse Ranch
.junipertrails.com

Sky Ranch Stables
skyranchstables.com

Fiddlestix Ranch
fiddlestixranch.com

Utah

Utah is a land for outdoor adventures and offers Equestrian Adventuresses a vast network of trails through four of the five National Parks in the state. The mountains offer a cool place to ride in the summer months.

Most riders head south the rest of the year due to the multitude of networked trails that go through serpentine canyons with hues of reds, oranges, yellows and lavenders.

Pro Tip

Hot Springs: For those of us that love hot springs soaking after a good riding adventure, Utah has at least five to choose from. Saratoga, Fifth Water, Mystic, Meadows Hot Springs and Gandy Warm Springs.

Viewing wild horses is a very unique aspect to Utah. There are 22 herds of wild mustangs that are protected in the state. This is an activity that requires some planning because most of the herds remain in remote areas away from civilization. Imagine watching a huge herd grazing with spirited foals playing in the vast unfenced valleys and hills. Mustangs are beautiful horses with an array of colors as wild as the horses themselves.

Native American Cultural Activities: Utah is another state that has a rich history with several of the Native American tribes. Each tribe has its own unique culture that can be seen in the art, ceremonies and clothing. From Petroglyphs on cave walls to basket weaving there are treasures to be found at some of the Heritage sites and markets.

Herding wild Bison. Perhaps the most exciting event for Equestrian Adventuresses is the Antelope Island Bison Round Up. Over 700 bison are rounded up and up to 200 riders can join in. Bison are up to 2000 pounds and can be pretty stubborn. These animals are to be dealt with professionally and the advanced herders must give you training on how to herd these giant animals.Riders are divided into teams and ride on the left or right flanks to keep the bison together.

Another 100 riders can follow in the rear of the group at a slower more relaxed pace. The breeder bulls are not rounded up as they are the difficult ones and are needed to remain. This is definitely an adventure that cannot be found anywhere else. The herd is helped by keeping the numbers from getting too high. Riders can sign up on-line in September and the roundup occurs in October. Riders must bring their own horse unless they can be a part of a local ranch that participates.

Utah

April - May
September - October

Where to Ride

Zion Canyon Trail Ride
ziontrailrides.com

Canyon Trail Rides
canyonrides.com

Ruby's Horseback Adventures
horserides.net

Hondoo Rivers & Trails
hondoo.com

Snow Canyon Trail Rides
snowcanyontrailrides.com

Rising K Ranch
risingkranchtrailrides.com

North Forty Escapes
northfortyescapes.com

Rocky Mountain Outfitters
rockymtnoutfitters.com

Other Books By Equestrian Adventuresses

Horse Riding in Every Country Catalog: Listings of over 400+ stables in over 180+ countries

Equestrian Adventuresses Series Book 1: Saddles and Sisterhood - True Stories of Friendships Built in the Saddle

Book 2: Going the Distance - True Stories of horse riders overcoming the odds while traveling on horseback

Book 3: Leg Up - True Stories of horse riders conquering extreme challenges around the world

Best in 2020 World Travel Guide for Equestrians

2020 Job Book: How to Work and Volunteer Abroad with Horses

All our books are available on Amazon Worldwide.
You may also find them at:
www.EquestrianAdventuresses.com

Learn from Krystal at:
https://linktr.ee/equestrianadventuresses

Learn from Krystal how to "Speak the Horse Language" no matter what country you travel to with the Equestrian Adventuresses Masterclass!

https://linktr.ee/equestrianadventuresses

Interested in Traveling the World on Horseback But Don't Know Where to Start?

What You'll Learn:

- How to Speak the Horse Language in ANY country
- How to be more confident on the ground and in the saddle with horses
- How to travel solo confidently
- Strategies to achieve your goals--no matter how big your dreams are
- How to gain your horse's trust and build their confidence
- Mastering your own body language
- What is "Energy" and how does it influence your horse
- How to stay safe while traveling as a solo woman
- How to read situations
- Effective strategies to turn your goals, ideas & dreams into ACTIONABLE PLANS
- And much, much more!

Learn from the comfort of your own home with this simple online video course!

https://linktr.ee/equestrianadventuresses

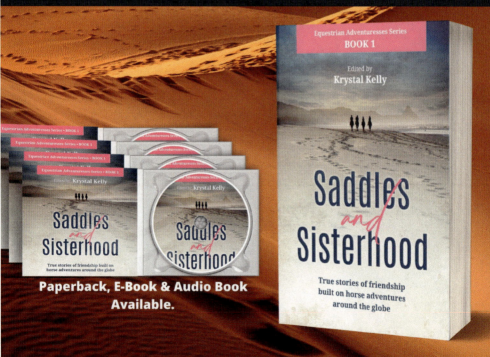

The best way to discover Argentina

Ampascachi Horse Riding Holidays
https://ampascachi.com

Made in the USA
Columbia, SC
15 August 2020

AUG   2020